Kofi Loves Music

By Dr. Artika Tyner

Text Copyright © 2020 Dr. Artika Tyner

Illustrations copyright © 2020 Planting People Growing Justice Press

Illustrations by Bilal Karaca
Design by Reyhana Ismail

All rights reserved.

No part of this book may be reproduced in any manner without express written consent of the publisher, except in the case of brief excerpts in critical reviews and articles.

All inquiries or sales request should be addressed to:

Planting People Growing Justice Press
P.O. Box 131894
Saint Paul, MN 55113
www.ppgjli.org

Printed and bound in the United States of America
First Edition
LCCN: 2020900130
SC ISBN: 978-0-9985553-5-5

Dedication

This book is dedicated to the children in Senchi Ferry, Ghana.
A.T.

Kofi loves music, family and unity.

Musical Instruments

Kalimba- thumb piano
Djembe- drum from West Africa
Balafon- gourd-resonated xylophone
Caxixi- basket shaped shaker
Udu- clay drum
Kora- stringed instrument; harp
Shekere- percussion instrument

Kofi loves music.

Grandpa and Kofi make music together.

One kalimba,

Grandpa plays with two hands.

Two kalimbas together,

Kofi makes a new harmony.

Three beats on the djembe drum.

Four beats on the balafon with a stick.

Five uncles

hear the music and join the fun.

Kofi smiles as they add new beats to the rhythm.

Six shakes of the caxixi.

Kofi claps his hands.

Kofi starts to dance.

Nine shakes of the shekere

Ten voices singing together.

About the Author

Dr. Artika R. Tyner (a.k.a. Miss Freedom Fighter, Esquire) is a passionate educator, an award-winning author, a civil rights attorney, a sought-after speaker, and an advocate for justice who is committed to helping children discover their leadership potential and serve as change agents in the global community. She is the founder/CEO of the Planting People Growing Justice LLC.

About Planting People Growing Justice Leadership Institute

Planting People Growing Justice Leadership Institute seeks to plant seeds of social change through education, training, and community outreach.

A portion of proceeds from this book will support the educational programming of Planting People Growing Justice Leadership Institute.

Learn more at www.ppgjli.org

Made in the USA
Monee, IL
12 March 2022